SKY HIGH
# NORFOLK BROADS
## AN AERIAL JOURNEY

**MIKE PAGE**

HALSGROVE

First published in Great Britain in 2008

**British Library Cataloguing-in-Publication Data**
A CIP record for this title is available from the British Library

ISBN 978 1 84114 701 7

HALSGROVE
Halsgrove House
Ryelands Industrial Estate
Bagley Road, Wellington
Somerset TA21 9PZ
Tel: 01823 653777
Fax: 01823 216796
email: sales@halsgrove.com
website: www.halsgrove.com

Printed and bound by D'Auria Industrie Grafiche, Italy

# Introduction

There is no better way to experience the unique landscapes of the Norfolk and Suffolk Broads than to see them from the air. And there is no better photographer than Mike Page to take you on this aerial journey. His bestselling books of aerial photography of Norfolk and Suffolk have delighted and informed thousands of readers.

In this book the reader is offered a visual memento of the Broads through photographs specially selected by the author. Both for those who know the Broads well, or for those who are visiting on holiday, this gem of a book provides the perfect keepsake.

Mike Page's books include: *A Broads Eye View; A Broads Eye View 2; The Norfolk Coast from the Air; The Suffolk Coast from the Air.*

Cockshoot Broad is linked to the River Bure by the narrow channel. Its name describes one of the activities which used to take place here.

The Broads were formed when medieval man dug out peat for his domestic needs.
The peat turves often were carted away by river.

Here silt is being pumped from part of Barnby Broad to help restore aquatic life.

Alderfen Broad is landlocked. Recently it has been mud pumped. A fish curtain divides the broad in an attempt to encourage zoo-plankton to thrive where no fish can eat them. Extra shelter is afforded the zoo-plankton by a grid of mesh with 'brushes' suspended in the water to provide a habitat. The water is now visibly clearer where the fish have been excluded.

Breydon Bridge lifts to allow tall masted boats through,
much to the annoyance of Yarmouth's road traffic sometimes!

Haddiscoe Island is formed by the River Yare to the left, the River Waveney to the right and the New Cut in the foreground. Breydon Water is in the background.

*Opposite:* On Fritton Lake nets used to be suspended across the broad and wildfowl driven into a mesh tunnel called a decoy. The catch was sent to Smithfield Market.

The village of Loddon is the end of navigation on the River Chet.

The staithe at Malthouse Broad is a very popular overnight mooring.

Most boats need a pilot to get them through the medieval Potter Heigham bridge.

*Opposite:* The River Ant winds its way past the village of Irstead (bottom right) and the How Hill Estate and Crome's Broad (left). The patchwork of colours are made by the reed marshes, the fen and the fields which have been drained for agriculture.

Reedham Swing Bridge. There's often a queue of boats
waiting for the railway bridge to open.

*Opposite:* Reedham.

The Yare navigation race.
The cruising club enjoying
a day on the River Yare.

*Opposite:*
Rockland Broad looking
east. Several old trading
wherries were sunk in
this broad when there
was no longer any work
for them.

The River Bure runs alongside Breydon Water.

The end of another perfect day over Hickling.

The fine city of Norwich at twilight, with Whitlingham Country Park in the foreground.

*Opposite:* Upton Broad looking north-west. Managed by the Norfolk Wildlife Trust, Upton Broad was once connected to the River Bure.

Autumn colours near Wroxham.

*Opposite:* Horning Upper Street.

Barton Regatta – an annual event each October.

A perfect day for racing on Barton Broad.

Barton Broad looks very different on a winter's day!

The Suffolk town of Beccles on the River Waveney.

Berney Arms Mill is the tallest drainage mill in The Broads. The sails
are now only for show, a mechanical pump drains the marshes today.
Downriver the Berney Arms pub is accessible to customers by water only.

The navigation channel across Breydon Water needs to be dredged regularly.

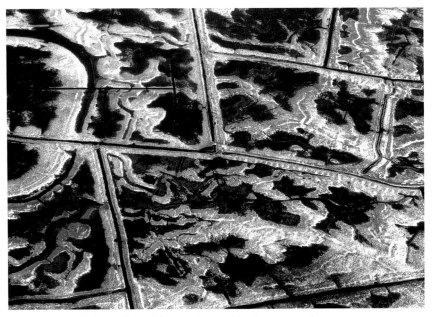

The stark lines of the dykes on Berney Marshes are in sharp contrast to the weird shapes made by the (slightly) higher snow covered areas.

There's an ongoing programme of scrub clearance, here willows are being grubbed out to maintain a traditional Broadland landscape.

*Opposite:* A low lying area and a flood tide at Brundall.

Twisting & turning.
No naturally formed
river runs in a dead
straight line.  Here, just
upriver of St Benet's
there's an abundance
of turns!

*Opposite:*
A gentle sail on
Hickling Broad.

Picture postcard beauty of How Hill on the River Ant.

*Opposite:* The outlines of the former buildings can be seen near the gatehouse of St Benet's Abbey as can the raised causeway walked by the monks on their way to St James' hospital in the next parish of Horning. The windmill in the gatehouse was built after the monks had left and the buildings had fallen down. Recent flood alleviation work has been undertaken upriver of the gatehouse along the rivers Bure and Ant.

How Hill house was built in 1903 by Edward Boardman as his family's home but it has been an environmental study centre for the last forty years.

*Opposite:* The River Wensum takes Waterborne traffic into the heart of Norwich.

Martham Broad with the coast just a couple of miles away.

Ashtree Farm Mill. Restoration was completed in 2007.
The mill was one of the last to work in Broadland.

Oulton Broad, with Lake Lothing and the sea off to the right through Mutford Lock.

Reedham Ferry. Crossing the River Yare on the ferry saves miles of driving but in summer there's often a wait to get to the head of the queue.

Quiet backwaters. Sunshine and a gentle breeze, just the opportunity for a quiet sail!

Ongoing flood alleviation work on the River Bure looking downstream toward Thurne mouth.

Riverside properties.
These houses have a
wonderful view across
Black Horse Broad,
also known as Hoveton
Little Broad

Locally grown reed will
have been used to
thatch all these roofs

43

Salhouse Broad with the River Bure and a corner of Hoveton Great Broad in the foreground.

The meandering River Waveney at St Olave's is joined by the dead straight New Cut before it flows past Somerleyton toward Oulton Broad and Beccles.

Surlingham to Bramerton. Surlingham Ferry used to cross the river where the pub which bears its name (foreground) still stands.

*Opposite:* The meeting of the Rivers Yare and Bure at Great Yarmouth.

A recent newcomer to The Broads is the *Southern Belle*
which runs river trips from Great Yarmouth.

*Opposite:* Whitlingham Great Broad looking towards the city. The broad
was formed when gravel was extracted for Norwich's Southern bypass.

Thurne Village. The River Thurne with Thurne Mill at the end of
Thurne Dyke and St Benet's Level mill on the opposite bank.

Thurne Regatta at Thurne Mouth. The River Bure makes a right-angled turn here!

Scrub clearance at Upton. A great deal of scrub clearance has been done here at Upton Broad, much of it by a volunteer workforce. Left unchecked the broadland scenery would quickly revert to consisting of water loving trees such as alder and willow.

*Opposite:* Trinity Broads. The Trinity Broads are Filby, Lily, Rollesby, Ormesby and Ormesby Little Broads – five of them!

The newly restored Turf Fen Mill at How Hill. Its original purpose was to drain the marshes.

Pleasure wherry *Hathor* was built in 1915 for the Colman sisters of Colman's Mustard fame.

The A47 road ('the Acle Straight'), the railway line and the River Bure all make their way to Great Yarmouth. The river takes its time!

Mixed craft. There are several traditional
wooden cruisers and sailing boats here
among their fibreglass successors!

*Opposite:* Wroxham with the village of
Hoveton on the far side of the bridge.

All the sailing dinghies have been put away leaving a tranquil Wroxham Broad.

Close to the sea. Horsey Mere, Martham and Hickling Broads are so close to the sea that a combination of strong onshore winds and high tides can present a danger of flooding.

The wonderful Fairhaven Gardens run down to the edge of South Walsham Inner Broad.

There's a wonderful view from the gallery at the top of Horsey windmill.

*Albion* is one of only two trading wherries still afloat. The distinctive black sail came about because wherrymen coated it with a mix of herring oil, soot and tar to make it last longer. The smell must have been overpowering!

Wayford Bridge on the River Ant marks the start of the North Walsham and Dilham Canal.

*Opposite:* Wroxham is where the boat hire industry first began at the turn of the twentieth century. There are over two hundred miles of waterways to explore.

Hickling Broad, the largest of the Broads